Home Grown Marketing Strategies That GROW Your Business

7 Free or Low Cost Tools That Cultivate More Cash

Lydia Harris

Home Grown Marketing Strategies That Grow Your Business
Copyright © 2010 by The Entrepreneurs' Garden, LLC.
ISBN **978-1-60702-207-7**

All rights reserved. No part of this book may be reproduced or transmitted in any form or by any means without written permission from the author.

Published in USA by The Entrepreneurs' Garden Press (www.TheEntrepreneursGarden.com)

Dedication

This book is dedicated to the new dreamers.

The new dreamers are those individuals that feel they have something to give to and share with the world, but can't quite see how to do it. Often armed with nothing more than their dream fueled by desire and passion, the new dreamers must learn how to use their creativity to acquire what many others can easily just buy.

These new dreamers have faith that if they just keep walking along the path they feel meant for them, that they will live in the abundance of their purpose fulfilled.

These new dreamers have belief that when living on purpose they can effect changes in the world as miraculous as the sunrise and as calming as the glow of the moon.

The Entrepreneurs' Garden proudly supports the visions of the new dreamers with The Home Grown Learning Series.

Contents

Dedication

Preface

Introduction

Tool Number 1 1

Tool Number 2 5

Tool Number 3 9

Tool Number 4 13

Tool Number 5 17

Tool Number 6 21

Tool Number 7 23

About The Entrepreneurs Garden 27

Our Gift to You 29

About the Author 31

Preface

This book was developed as part of The Entrepreneurs' Garden Home Grown Learning Series to supplement the development of cost effective and purpose driven marketing systems for new and seasoned entrepreneurs.

I would love to say that all of these tools are brand new to the marketplace and that you are among the first to know about them, but that is not the case. Like shovels used in a garden, when you need to dig a hole, a shovel is generally what you would use to achieve that end result. The key is to use a small shovel when you need a small hole, a snow shovel when you want to move snow, or the knowledge that whatever you need to dig, you select the most appropriate shovel to get the job done.

Similarly, the tools for marketing are basic. Variety within each tool set is what you need (or develop) for specific purposes and needs. There is no need to reinvent the wheel here, but there is great benefit to better understanding how we can creatively select and use traditional tools to do new jobs more effectively.

Introduction

"You are surrounded by simple, obvious solutions that can dramatically increase your income, power, influence and success. The problem is you just don't see them." ~ Jay Abraham

"The new economy" has frightened many with the financial impact in our families and businesses. This guide was developed to acknowledge the emerging relationship based environment that can become profitable with simple cost effective tools.

In times when most businesses are cutting back on marketing expenditures, it does not have to mean that one cuts back on the actual practice of marketing. We must just become more creative.

Home Grown Marketing Strategies That Grow Your Business is a guide to exploration of how business owners can actually expand their marketing efforts with surprisingly little cost. In most cases, utilization of these seven simple tools (and there are so many more) can recharge and energize any entrepreneurs' marketing plan.

Each tool is one of seven of the most important words to a growing business, no matter what your size or net worth. They all begin with the letter "C" by choice to represent the ultimate benefits to your business that you can easily "see".

Those seven "C" words that define each of the Home Grown Marketing Strategies in order of their presentation in this book are:

1. Creativity
2. Connection
3. Credibility
4. Collaboration

5. Clarity
6. Consistency
7. Commitment

The utilization of these tools is scalable. Here we offer FREE and low cost strategies that can easily be expanded upon with additional funding for accelerated and enhanced results. But for now, right here, you can begin in most cases, for FREE.

We still have a great amount of work to do in social development, including resolving one of the biggest challenges we face in this area, namely, reducing the gap between high-income earners and people, citizens of our country, who are still living on very modest means indeed. But we cannot, of course, adopt the solution used 80 years ago and simply confiscate the riches of some to redistribute among others. We will use completely different means to resolve this problem, namely, we will ensure good economic growth. ~ Vladimir Putin

Welcome to The Entrepreneurs' Garden!

Tool Number One
The Power of Creativity

"If the circus is coming to town and you paint a sign saying, "Circus is coming to Fairgrounds Sunday," that's Advertising. If you put the sign on the back of an elephant and walk him through town, that's Promotion. If the elephant walks through the Mayors' flower bed, that's Publicity. If you can get the Mayor to laugh about it, that's Public Relations. And if you planned the whole thing, that's Marketing." ~Anonymous

This was the best introduction and explanation of these terms I had ever seen. In my mind, Advertising, Promotion, Publicity, Public Relations and Marketing were all the same before I read this quote. I hope it is as clarifying for you as it was for me.

If nothing else, it leads nicely into the first of the seven tools included in this book to help you to create your own home grown strategies for marketing at little to no cost.

First let me explain a little about the "home grown" concept. The Entrepreneurs' Garden was founded on the premise that many of the tools used to create and grow a sustainable, enjoyable and purpose driven business are not as elusive as most would think.

Many people believe that in order to start a business, lots of money has to be involved or invested. In many cases that is true, but in so many more, nothing could be further from the truth.

In fact, most big businesses were born of small, humble beginnings.

When I decided to move my family from Detroit, MI to Fort Lauderdale, FL in 2005, we (my mom and 2 sons) shipped the furniture and took the

1200 mile scenic southbound drive on I-75 almost from one end to the other. Along the way, we stopped in the unique very small town of Corbin, Kentucky. And what you ask made that such an interesting place? It was the birthplace of the original Kentucky Fried Chicken.

I would never have stopped in Corbin, Kentucky but they did something that made me and perhaps hundreds of thousands of people through the years do. Something that you can easily do in your business if you get creative and understand the value it can provide for you now and in the years to come.

And it can be free or at little cost.

What did this town do? It began simply with a sign and a listing in a book that I bought for the trip. The book listed quirky and unique stops along the I-75 corridor from one end to the other. My trip included most of the route making that of interest to me in my desire to break up the boredom for 2 kids and a grandma on a long road trip. They put their information where I would need it, when I would need it to get my attention.

Home Grown Marketing Strategy Tool #1 is to Get Their Attention. There are so many cost effective ways to get attention, you are only limited by the power of creativity. Many people start with signs, ads and other marketing materials that can be expensive or very low cost. The free tools can simply be how you present yourself to others in what you say, do or wear as you meet others for the first time.

Just as the book and sign were initially used to direct me to the KFC birthplace, and the sign advertising the circus, they both were attention getters. You can't sell anything to anyone unless you get their attention first. You have to show them that you have something for them.

Many times, we aren't aware of what we need. So there is no reason to be excited that you have it. But when you present your products or services creatively, even the people that didn't know they need it will remember. Because you got their attention.

For example, I planned a road trip and did not set out to find just another KFC. But once I saw it, I thought it might be a great tidbit of history for my family to experience. So because they were listed in a book specifically designed for someone like me making this I-75 trek, I included it in my plans. I timed it to coincide with grandmas' need for a bathroom break and lunch for the boys. It met my needs before I really knew I had them.

Advertising met promotion and publicity. I had an "a-ha" moment.
What alliances are you cultivating that will put you in touch with future customers? Are your signs clearly displayed where potential new customers will be?

It all starts with getting the attention of your current and potential customers. Great attention getters are one of the most powerful marketing tools and can have long lasting effects.

"The only limit to your impact is your imagination and commitment."
~ Anthony Robbins

Tool Number Two:
The Power of Connection

Thoreau said: "I know of no more encouraging fact than the unquestioned ability of a man to elevate his life by conscious endeavor." That is not only an encouraging statement; it is also an empowering one. It means you can accomplish a lot by applying your brainpower and then moving forward with it. ~ Donald Trump

Once you have their attention, you have got to quickly engage your potential customer or business associate into wanting to learn more. Whether it is on your website, business card or when you meet someone in person, that next few seconds are critical in solidifying your first impression.

Many of us have had the experience where we met someone and they leave us feeling like we want to connect with them. They leave us with that feeling that they have something that we could benefit from in the form of expertise, connections or good will. Isn't this how you want people to feel when they meet you?

By now most of us have had the opportunity to visit a website or two. In fact, with the burgeoning of technology, you often can't connect with people in person at major companies; they usually direct you first to their website. So for the small business owner, this tool becomes another dimension of you and your business.

When you look at a website, as it opens what do you see, think or feel? Is it pleasing to the eye? Can you read the text easily and understand the written message? Does it make you want to learn more about the company? Do you think "WOW" or do you get lost in trying to figure out where to go or what to do to get what you came to the site for?

This same range of reactions occurs not only with your visual media, but also with YOU.

So when you meet someone, do you notice the things you see, think or feel? Absolutely! Your verbal and non-verbal presentation is evaluated in mere seconds, just like your website.

Home Grown Marketing Strategy #2 is your Communication Impact. The power of connection is launched by how others see you and what they think about what you say. They also determine how you make them feel. And the best part is that your communication style, impact and delivery is totally controlled by you and is **FREE**!

Many of you know that prior to growing my entrepreneurial garden; I have a long career as a Registered Nurse. My communication needs were driven by that vocation and my family/friends, which did not require the skills that my business does. When I realized my growth needs in this area, I sought information on how to be a more effective communicator. This part unfortunately was not free, but I did find some low cost options to fulfill my needs.

Initially, I invested in courses on public speaking given by local business owners that I knew, trusted and respected with wonderful results. However, maintaining long term training efforts grew more expensive. Though I love and plan to utilize the services of a private or small group coach in the future, I found my most cost effective communication training at a local Toastmasters International Club.

At this writing, I have been a member for almost nine months and am just a few weeks away from completion of my first designation as a Competent Communicator by an internationally recognized organization that promotes the art of public speaking. Since I desired to learn more about promotion and public relations, I was recently elected as the Vice President of Public Relations of my local club. So of course, I must include this resource for you. www.toastmasters.org

Though it involves weekly meetings and service work without pay as part of the leadership training program, joining Toastmasters has been one of the most empowering decisions, and cost effective training (and networking) investments I have made in my personal growth and development to enhance my communication impact.

With that being said, we must all be mindful that the words we say are just a small percentage of what leaves an impression on others. Just as many are familiar with the expression that "people do business with people they know like and trust" we must have the realization that our own individuality and authenticity is the most significant driving force in our ability to connect with others.

"In the last analysis, what we are communicates far more eloquently than anything we say or do." ~ Stephen R. Covey

Tool Number Three
The Power of Credibility

If money is your hope for independence you will never have it. The only real security that a man will have in this world is a reserve of knowledge, experience, and ability. ~ Henry Ford

When I began this entrepreneurial journey in 2008, I had been quite confident of who I was and what I did in my nursing career. My resume and bio had evolved over the years, and it was easy for me to share information about myself and what I did in that context.

When I completed my first book, *"**How You Gonna Pay for Those Shoes?**"* in the summer of 2008, I realized that people were expecting me to talk about it in order to determine if they wanted to buy it. The thought of preparing for that never crossed my mind - I had been consumed with the struggle just to complete it!

As I began to tell people about the book, I could see them thinking the message of the book was a good idea, but not wanting to listen to my lengthy explanation about it. Fortunately at about the same time I was introduced to a method of clear, concise, powerful and quick info sharing to communicate while creating interest rather than boredom. Many thanks go out to Lisa Nichols and my CEO Space family for introducing me to these concepts. Though I may still have a long way to go, I at least know the road to take. And when you can save time by taking the right road, you also save money, not to mention frustration.

I learned that I had to begin to develop my "non-nurse" persona as an author and businesswoman. Talk about scary!

I began a self-assessment tour that has led me to develop credibility in this new arena, which also led to public self-disclosure. But without credibility, how could I seek trust and relationship development from those I would like to know me, and like me enough to become my valued customers?

In my nursing career, my resume was primarily seen by those I was seeking employment from or to align with in specific business transactions. In this new career, I had to go on Facebook, LinkedIn, Twitter and more before millions of people, most I would never even know, and disclose my information. Yikes!

It took a little while for me to accept that this was now the new norm for business. Then as I continued along the journey, I realized that though it would be necessary to present myself to the public, I still had control over what I shared and how. And now I understand that one of the keys to revealing oneself to the world is to create that unveiling in a manner that is in alignment with all of the intended uses of the information. All of the messages I created had to be compatible.

Home Grown Marketing Tool #3 was my Personal Expertise Package (PEP). This tool takes your potential customer from their first point of awareness that you exist all the way through your entire relationship with them!

Recently popularized is the acronym for what any potential (or current) customer thinks when you have any kind of contact with them. In fact it has been called the radio station everyone listens to and from their perception is based: WII.FM – What's In It For Me. So from seeing your website, Facebook profile, or marketing flyer to meeting you at a networking event with hand outstretched to shake or present a business card, this is the immediate thought.

When we read something written about or by someone, or hear them speak, it is not uncommon to have a thought about how connecting with them would have some benefit? Nothing to be ashamed of, just a lesson learned that reveals the need to prepare for to get in profit from the game of marketing. This is where your PEP comes in handy.

With your prepared PEP, you have already considered the WII.FM perspective of all you meet and are empowered to quickly, authentically and comfortably respond to all inquiries. If your messages are not all the same, you will leave people confused. Customers that get mixed messages don't buy. Once you get the attention of your customer, you want all of your communications to be clear, impactful, authentic and quick in how they illustrate your credibility and the benefits of connecting to you.

Your PEP includes all of your communications about you and the products/services you provide. Examples of your PEP are found in your:
1. Elevator speech
2. Social networking profiles and posts
3. Bio snippets like in your "About Me" website section
4. Public speaking messages
5. Product demonstrations
6. Writing articles about your business
7. Business and sales letters
8. Testimonials
9. Guarantees

Your expertise includes life experiences and skills that may have been obtained in non-traditional source. You don't have to have a college degree, but whatever you have, you must show your customer that it is valuable to them and solves their problem. Testimonials from happy customers are a great confirmation of your expertise.

"Your earning ability today is largely dependent upon your knowledge, skill and your ability to combine that knowledge and skill in such a way that you contribute value for which customers are going to pay."
~ Brian Tracy

Tool Number Four
The Power of Collaboration

"The more I help others to succeed, the more I succeed."
~ Ray Kroc

Many new small business owners believe that if there is limited funding available for assistance with projects that they will have to do all of the work themselves. Though it can be said that you need either money or time to begin a business venture, it is critical that you understand the role that leverage can play in getting things done with time efficiency and cost effectiveness.

Most marketers use the power of collaboration to leverage what they have into multiples of options. For example, many writers like me spend a lot of time trying to sell their books to the people they know or come into contact with. In this fashion, I would only be able to sell to a limited number of people.

When I enlisted the aid of others to assist me in selling my books for a piece of the profit, then I gain a greater potential customer base with the use of leverage. Though my profit may not be as great on a per book basis because I have to split it with a third party, I would have more profit as more books are being sold than I was able to sell alone without the collaboration of others.

Home Grown Marketing Strategy #4 is to Promote or Refer the Products and/or Services of Others. This can be done in person via networking. It can also be done online with website sales tools.

I first discovered the power of this strategy by accident. I had discovered a local networking group and began to bond with the organizers and friends I was making. I began to refer people that joined this group that I couldn't afford to join myself! But I attended the meetings as a non-member because I met some incredible people that were inspiring to me in my transition from nurse to entrepreneur.

Shortly thereafter, the group held their first major event and of course needed help with some of the last minute details. I was available and spent the evening prior to the event working into the wee hours of the morning with them. I was struggling financially at the time having recently lost my job and couldn't afford to continue my membership. My unconditional service and referrals so impressed them that without knowing my financial situation, they offered me a free membership! This was perhaps the first time in my life that I saw the Pay it Forward spirit in action.

And I have lived by it ever since. Not just to receive, but because it just makes since. You cannot reap the harvest unless you plant the seed for the crop.

So at most of my events and on my websites you will see information about other businesses, events and opportunities. I align my public promotion of others with my own topics and in many cases create joint ventures. The importance and value of TEAM cannot be stressed enough. In a coaching class with Mark Victor Hansen I will never forget him telling us that the power of TEAM is **<u>T</u>ogether <u>E</u>veryone <u>A</u>chieves <u>M</u>iracles**.

And miracles happen when you help others. Just begin to refer to others unconditionally and watch the miracles unfold. People remember someone who referred them a new client, or who sent them some critical information to enhance their business. Most will then want to learn more about you to determine if they can assist you.

Bartering opportunities also can arise from these TEAM concepts. And for the fiscally challenged entrepreneur, developing ways to meet your growing needs without cash expenditures are golden. I have bartered for many things in my short journey that have served me perhaps greater than if I had a customer to make a purchase. I get great feedback with my exchange, testimonials to use in my promotions, practice to confirm my ability to do as I promise, and ambassadors who share their positive experiences with others when the results of our association are evident to the public.

And a beautiful (and profitable) cycle begins…..

"I have found no greater satisfaction than achieving success through honest dealing and strict adherence to the view that, for you to gain, those you deal with should gain as well." ~ Alan Greenspan

Tool Number Five
The Power of Clarity

"When you're really trying to make serious change, you don't want people to get caught up in emotion because change isn't emotion. Its real work and organization and strategy and that's just the truth of it. I mean, you pull people in with inspiration, but then you have to roll up your sleeves and you've got to make sacrifices and you have got to have structure." ~ Michelle Obama

In the previous chapters, you have looked at how you get the attention of your customers with impactful communications and collaborating testimony that confirm your credibility as the person they want to help them with the services you provide. Now it is time to make sure that you are getting all of this information to the right people.

I spent many months telling people about my projects, hearing from most of them what a good set of ideas I had. I became very good at engaging people in conversations about my vision, but I was missing one very important step.

Though I was familiar with the WII.FM concept mentioned in Tool Number Three, I never used that to tell others how my services and products would be of benefit to them in a compelling manner. It was at this time that I also realized my lack of experience in developing a "call to action" or "closing the sale".

So back to the books and workshops I went. They serve me well, but there comes a point where "information saturation" results in a loss of focus on what is really needed to move forward. There are so many people that I met by this time that had used a variety of methods. All I wanted was what worked. No longer did I just want what was fun, pleasant and gave me warm fuzzies, I wanted results!

I would love to say I wrote this book in the sequence of how I started my business but I cannot. It is purely a hindsight production. I realized very late in the game some critical pieces I had not been attentive to that were necessary for me to move on. So that meant change was in order.

I thought it was because I did not have certain "skills". In the nursing world, either you know how to start an IV or you don't. I thought I wasn't selling my book because I didn't know how to sell. Though to some degree that was true, but more importantly it was because I had not clearly identified who my ideal customer was so that I could speak primarily to them about my products and services.

It has now evolved into a group of buzz terms:
- ideal customer
- target market
- best prospect
- and many more creatively stated phrases

And until I simplified the definition of this elusive group of businesses and individuals, I could not grow my business to meet my desired revenue model until I became clear on this.

Home Grown Marketing Tool #5 is a <u>WRITTEN</u> Marketing Plan. To derive the greatest benefit from any strategy developed to meet a goal, a written plan with tactics to meet each strategy is absolutely necessary.

The marketing plan is a dynamic document that grows and is amended as goals are achieved and failing strategies and tactics are replaced with more effective ones. It defines who you are, what you do, your products/services and your time/dollar budgets that are set aside just for marketing.

Your marketing plan goes into greater details to describe your target market, including their description and demographics. It also clarifies how you will reach them, what tools you will use to do so, and at what frequency. In researching your ideal customer, you learn what they like so that you can make better connections with them. You need to get crystal clear on what their problems are and they need so that you can offer those solutions to them.

One might think that if I wanted to market to nurses, that I could go to a women's group or a health provider convention. That didn't work. I had to go specifically to nurses groups. Then I learned that I didn't need to go to all nurses groups. There are subspecialties that are far more entrepreneurial minded than others. I learned from group discussions, surveys (that have already been done) and other research strategies more about that market. Now I am able to build a more effective platform in which to share myself through my PEP, collaborations and creativity because of clarity.

I never thought of myself as a marketer and that was one of my first and biggest mistakes. If I don't market myself and my products/services, then who will? No one knows me like me. No one can answer questions about me like me. I can't afford to pay someone to study me and promote me to the world – yet. So until then, marketing me is up to me. Like it or not, I am a marketer. And if I don't like it, I won't be able to grow a profitable business.
Once I achieved clarity about how my services and products benefit others, I became much better at sharing how my story is theirs. Then I continue the progression on how my solutions can also be theirs as well.

I will be a marketing student throughout my business life to keep current with trends and tactics that I include in my marketing plan. Now I am beginning to love it and be happily driven by it. No longer just for the money (though that is a huge motivator and ultimately how I can objectively measure my business success) but for the legacy I will leave; the foot print of my teachings on the lives they will impact across the globe and the chronology of time.

"We must have a theme, a goal, a purpose in our lives. If you don't know where you're aiming, you don't have a goal. My goal is to live my life in such a way that when I die, someone can say, she cared."
~ Mary Kay Ash

Tool Number Six
The Power of Consistency

"If you want to be successful in a particular field of endeavor, I think perseverance is one of the key qualities. It's very important that you find something that you care about, that you have a deep passion for, because you're going to have to devote a lot of your life to it."
~ George Lucas

Now armed with a killer marketing plan, a dynamic PEP, ever improving communication skills, a growing network of alliances and customers, I move onward to the next step.

Each of the preceding tools are valuable independently and grow exponentially more so when used collectively, however, without this tool, none of the others will exist or remain profitable for long. Not only must you be consistent in utilizing the aforementioned tools, there remains another key to truly unlock the massive potential that can be realized from all of your planning.

You can have the greatest of ideas, but without this special IDEA you will not move forward.

Home Grown Marketing Strategy #6 is the power of Implementing Daily Evolutionary Actions. Without action, your plans are just journals of unfulfilled dreams that will never be birthed into reality. Without consistent, purposeful action, you will not achieve your goals.
Your actions on the tactics you have outlined for each of your marketing strategies hold the key to your success. Without implementing your

plans through a consistent and determined course of action, you cannot grow a business.

The process of transformation from unemployed and underemployed to rewarding income generation requires evolution. Your mind, thoughts, emotions, behaviors and activities have to evolve from where you are, to where you want to be. Without daily attention to the process it will take much longer and the success rate for achievement of the outcome is reduced by distraction and eventually disbelief.

Entrepreneurship requires that you work diligently in the face of adversity, delayed gratification and often failure. You have to push yourself past points where you previously stopped, perhaps due to fear.

You have to be consistently committed to the evolutionary process that will change your habits and propel you beyond your limiting beliefs to the realization of your dreams. It is as simple as the concept of an IDEA.

The successful person makes a habit of doing what the failing person doesn't like to do. ~ Thomas Edison

Tool Number Seven
The Power of Commitment

"The real source of wealth and capital in this new era is not material things. It is the human mind, the human spirit, the human imagination, and our faith in the future" ~ Steve Forbes

Finally, we have reached the point in our development of Home Grown Marketing Strategies That Grow Your Business where we must realize that all worthy and value based goals are achieved over a period of time. And this alludes to the fact that patience might come in handy in order to make our last "C" tool more palatable.

No plan is a good plan in absence of commitment to it. If you will not commit to your plans, dreams and the work necessary to grow them into a reality, then don't quit your day job. Success as an entrepreneur will elude you as will any possibility of getting any cash out of the deal. You must plan the work necessary to overcome barriers and reach goals and commit to doing the work required to harvest the desired results.

So it is not money that you need to hire consultants and buy flashy marketing materials that will ensure your success. You don't need assistants and offices to start the growth of a successful entrepreneurial garden. You just need seeds and a place to grow. And the seeds are within you.

When you develop a business model to grow an enterprise that will provide you with financial freedom, you are really planting the seed of something that inspires you. This seed firmly planted in your spirit grows in your mind and imagination, giving you the faith that Steve

Forbes speaks of in the quote above. You are growing something that becomes a message you want to share with the world. So beginning with the end in mind, you have to give it away in order for it to grow into a harvest cultivated by the other tools we have discussed thus far.

Home Grown Marketing Strategy #7 is Giving. The seed cannot grow in your hand. You must give it the soil to grow in its' ideal environment. The ideal environment for any business to grow is in the hand and heart of its' customer. So you begin by committing to give to your customers so that they will be able to:

1. understand your creativity
2. make a connection
3. believe in your credibility and ability to serve them
4. experience the benefits of collaborating with you
5. see your vision with clarity
6. feel that you will consistently be of service to them
7. and sense your unwavering commitment to help them achieve their goals through the use of your given products and services.

The best use of this strategy I've heard was through a principle called Pink Spoon Marketing. It was popularized by one of my favorite businesses that I have supported for many years – Baskin Robbins.

When you go into a Baskin Robbins 31 Flavors ice cream store, they have these little pink spoons that they will give you samples of various ice cream flavors with. It would seem that if you and the store operator had time that you could taste all 31 if you were so inclined (though I never have). But the interesting thing that happens is that I always bought more than what I initially planned because there was so much that I liked, I either bought more then, or made a conscious effort to come back soon to get more later.

One tiny pink spoon turned me into a customer over and over again for many years. Your giving to your customer can become your pink spoon.

Having people buy from you once is good. Providing them with the opportunity to buy from you multiple times over years is priceless. When you can orchestrate it all from beginning with your creativity like the sign with the circus, to the end with the pink spoon, that my friends is the true spirit of Home Grown Marketing Strategies That Grow Your Business.

About The Entrepreneurs' Garden

"I'm a big believer in growth. Life is not about achievement, it's about learning and growth, and developing qualities like compassion, patience, perseverance, love, and joy, and so forth. And so if that is the case, then I think our goals should include something which stretches us."
~ Jack Canfield

The Entrepreneurs' Garden assists business owners and individuals across the globe with the development of Home Grown Strategies That Grow a Business.

With consulting services and guides to develop each component, you can feel confident having this "PEP in your step" toward confirmation of your credibility as an entrepreneur with integrity, intelligence and ingenuity.

The Entrepreneurs' Garden, LLC. creates and shares value based information that guides the growth of your life or world changing ideas and visions from seed to harvest.

Through publications, seminars, strategic alliances, consulting and referral marketing, The Entrepreneurs' Garden (TEG) is an emissary of enlightenment for you to "grow" what you need to excel in your personal, vocational and charitable endeavors.

TEG is a global initiative therefore many of the most utilized resources are digital. We offer publications (audio, video and print), seminars, consulting services and referrals. So no matter where you are, or what time it is, you can have access to a garden of resources for the growth of your projects.

Our publications cover business and personal development topics. From audio to zesty Facebook connecting, we have the information to guide you through acres of opportunity, one crop at a time.

We also have specialized development programs for nurses and young adult entrepreneurs desiring to grow into more effective CEO level leaders.

Our corporate philanthropy efforts support organizations that impact the lives of nurses, youth/young adults ages 12 - 26, animal rescue, and our nation's military/veterans.

Our mission is to guide young adults, nurses, veterans, baby boomers and other small/new business owners in the exploration and development of their passion driven ideas as income generators. This provides the tools to cultivate a cause or grow the seeds of ideas into the harvest of income or innovation.

The Entrepreneurs' Garden would love to stay connected with you through your choice of mediums. Grab a pink spoon online at:

www.TheEntrepreneursGarden.com
www.Facebook.com/TheEntrepreneursGarden

"Money is only used for two things. One, it's to make you comfortable, and the more comfortable you are the more creative you will become. And the other purpose is it enables you to extend the service you provide far beyond your own presence."
~ Bob Proctor

Our Gifts To You

"Let us not be satisfied with just giving money. Money is not enough, money can be got, but they need your hearts to love them. So, spread your love everywhere you go." ~ Mother Teresa

Thank you for the attention you have given us in the exploration of Home Grown Marketing Strategies That Grow Your Business: 7 FREE and Low Cost Tools That Cultivate More Cash.

Our corporate goals include philanthropic missions that include not just giving to organizations, but also giving back to you, our supporters. After all, you are a primary partner in our growth strategies as we share our messages across the globe. We want to honor that trust you have placed in us with the following "pink spoon" gifts:

1. For your creativity, we are including the link to a cool YouTube video that captures the spirit of the entrepreneur.
2. Emphasizing the power of connections, connect to a local Meet-Up group and Toastmasters for FREE.
3. A Social Media Calendar Worksheet to organize your posts, Tweets and other communications
4. Affirmations have been of great assistance to promote clarity and focus necessary to develop effective tactics for the strategies in all of my plans. Here are my top 7 affirmations that inspire "the marketer" in me.
5. When you are fully committed you realize that you have more than enough and should share. Our "pink spoon" for you exemplifies my favorite giveaways; all of them are included in this report, Promote Your Business with Home Grown Giveaways.

Again, we are honored to have been given the opportunity to share some of your time with this publication. Your gifts (and many more) are available at the corporate website and on Facebook:

http://TheEntrepreneursGarden.com
https://www.facebook.com/TheEntrepreneursGarden

Also included you will find a link to a survey so that I can learn more about how we can be of assistance to you during the growth of your entrepreneurial garden. Another free gift awaits you for taking the time to participate.

Please don't hesitate to contact us if you would like additional copies of this guide to share as gifts.

"To grow a successful business, you must first grow yourself."
~ Lydia Harris

About the Author

As the founder and CEO of The Entrepreneurs' Garden, LLC, Lydia continues to emerge as a change agent dedicated to cultivating your growth as a budding entrepreneur.

As a Registered Nurse specializing in Pediatrics, Mental Health, Rehabilitation and Medical Case Management for 30+ years (10 as an independent consultant), Lydia Harris has a long history as a professional nurturer, educator, motivator and problem solver.

Lydia currently makes her home near Ft. Lauderdale, Florida with her youngest son Benjamin and her 90+ years young mother, and continues to work as a RN.

Connect with Lydia here:
http://www.linkedin.com/in/lydiaharris
http://www.facebook.com/golydia

www.ingramcontent.com/pod-product-compliance
Lightning Source LLC
Chambersburg PA
CBHW020957180526
45163CB00006B/2401